Ancient Kriya Yoga Mission : Highly Recommended Books

(कूटस्थित दिव्यचक्षुदर्शित भाष्य श्रृंखला)

UNLOCKING HANUMAN CHALISA : REVELATIONS OF A HOUSEHOLDER MYSTIC
(हनुमान चालीसा कुंजिका : एक रहस्यवादी गृहस्थ का आत्मपुंज)
by
CHANDRA SHEKHAR KUMAR

DRINK AIR THERAPY TO KILL DIABETES
(A PATH TO SELF-CURE AND IMMORTALITY)
by CHANDRA SHEKHAR KUMAR

Lahiri Mahasaya

॥ ॐ नमः शिवाय॥

ॐ त्र्यम्बकं यजामहे सुगन्धिं पुष्टिवर्धनम्।
उर्वारुकमिव बंधनान्मृत्योर्मुक्षीय मामृतात्॥

ISBN-13: 978-1496113603
ISBN-10: 1496113608

email : ancientkriyayoga@gmail.com

Preface

This is a scriptural commentary of Lahiri Mahasaya on Kabir Gita in the Light of Kriya in which is a **conversation between Lord Dattatreya and Saint Kabir**. In the dialogue, *Dattatreya* asked *Kabir* the following six questions regarding the eleven subjects mind, breath, sound, *Prana* (life Force), *Brahma* (the ultimate Self), *Hang Sa* (Eternity), Time, Void, *Jiva* (individuality), Siva (Tranquility) and *Niranjana* (Unmanifestation):

1. What is mind ?

2. Where does mind exist ?

3. In the absence of heart, where does mind reside ?

4. What is the essence of mind ?

5. From where does mind spring ?

6. How is mind dissolved ?

Lahiri Mahasaya is a polestar of Kriya Yoga, a direct disciple of Mahavataar Babaji. In previous birth, he was Kabir. He is the Sadguru of Saint Shirdi Sai Baba.

For suggestions, feedback and comments, the author can be contacted at :
ancientkriyayoga@gmail.com

Ancient Kriya Yoga Mission
March 2, 2014

List of Chapters

Chapter 1

What is mind ?

Dattatreya : *What is the definition of mind?*

Kabir : **Restlessness.**

Dattatreya : *What is Air?*

Kabir : **Union.**

Dattatreya : *What is Sound?*

Kabir : **Air.**

Dattatreya : *What is Prana (life force)?*

Kabir : **Niranjana (Unmanifestation).**

Dattatreya : *What is Brahma (the Ultimate Self?*

Kabir : **Kindness.**

Dattatreya : *What is Hang Sa?*
Kabir : **Eternity.**

Dattatreya : *What is Time?*
Kabir : **Breath.**

Dattatreya : *What is the Void?*
Kabir : *(Remains Silent).*

Dattatreya : *What is individuality (jiva)?*
Kabir : *(Remains Silent).*

Dattatreya : *Who is Lord Siva?*
Kabir : *(Remains Silent).*

Dattatreya : *Who is Niranjana?*

Kabir : *(Remains Silent).*

Chapter 2

Where does mind exist?

Dattatreya : *Where lies the mind?*

Kabir : **At the Heart.**

Dattatreya : *Where lies the Air?*

Kabir : **At the Navel.**

Dattatreya : *Where lies Sound?*

Kabir : **In Anahat.**

Dattatreya : *Where lies Prana?*

Kabir : **In Niranjana.**

Dattatreya : *Where lies Brahma?*

Kabir : **Brahma lies in Brahma.**

Dattatreya : *Where lies Hang Sa?*

Kabir : *(Remains Silent).*

Dattatreya : *Where does time lie?*

Kabir : **In the lotus.**

Dattatreya : *Where does the Void lie?*

Kabir : **In Anup/Anupa/Anupam (Unmanifestation).**

Dattatreya : *Where does individuality lie?*

Kabir : *(Remains Silent).*

Dattatreya : *Where lies Siva?*

Kabir : *(Remains Silent).*

Dattatreya : *Where lies Niranjana?*

Kabir : **In the Spinal Cord.**

Chapter 3

In the Absence of Heart, where does the mind reside?

Dattatreya : *If there is no Heart, where can the mind reside?*

Kabir : In that case, the mind can reside in *Anupa* (Unmanifestation).

Dattatreya : *If there is no navel, where can the air reside?*

Kabir : In that case, air can reside in *Niranjana.*

Dattatreya : *If there is no* Anahat, *where can Sound reside?*

Kabir : In that case, Sound can reside in **Anupam** (Unmanifestation).

Dattatreya : *If there is no* Anahat, *where can Sound reside?*

Kabir : In that case, Sound can reside in **Anupam** (Unmanifestation).

Dattatreya : *If there is no Niranjana, where can Prana reside?*

Kabir : Then, Prana can reside in Eternity.

Dattatreya : *If there is no world, where can Brahma reside?*

Kabir : In that case, Brahma can reside in the inner Light.

Dattatreya : *If there is no sky, where can Hang Sa reside?*

Kabir : In that case, Hang Sa can reside in Eternity.

Dattatreya : *If there is no lotus, where can Time reside?*

Kabir : In that case, Time can reside in the Void.

Dattatreya : *If there is no formlessness, where can the Void reside?*

Kabir : In that case, the Void can reside in Omkar.

Dattatreya : *If there is no Air, where can individuality reside?*

Kabir : If there is no Air, individuality can reside in Lord Shiva.

Dattatreya : *If there is no moon, where can Lord Siva reside?*

Kabir : In that case, Tranquility can reside in Unmanifestation.

Dattatreya : *If there is no Spinal Cord, where can Niranjana reside?*

Kabir : **If there is no Spinal Cord, Niranjana can reside in Brahma.**

Chapter 4

Essence of The Mind

Dattatreya : *What is the essence of the mind?*

Kabir : **Air.**

Dattatreya : *What is the essence of breath?*

Kabir : **Renunciation.**

Dattatreya : *What is the essence of renunciation?*

Kabir : **It is inner Sound.**

Dattatreya : *What is the essence of Sound?*

Kabir : **Prana is the essence of Sound.**

Dattatreya : *What is the essence of Prana?*

Kabir : **It is Brahma.**

Dattatreya : *What is the essence of Brahma?*

Kabir : **It is Hang Sa.**

Dattatreya : *What is the essence of Hang Sa?*

Kabir : **It is Eternity.**

Dattatreya : *What is the essence of Time?*

Kabir : **It is Tranquility.**

Dattatreya : *What is the essence of Tranquility?*

Kabir : **It is Niranjana.**

Dattatreya : *What is the essence of Niranjana?*

Kabir : **It is One Brahma.**

Chapter 5

Source of The Mind

Dattatreya : *From where is Niranjana produced?*

Kabir : **From Fire.**

Dattatreya : *From where is Siva produced?*
Kabir : **From Niranjana.**

Dattatreya : *From where is jiva (individuality) produced?*
Kabir : **From Siva (Tranquility).**

Dattatreya : *From where is the Void produced?*

Kabir : It is produced from Omkar.

Dattatreya : *From where is Time produced?*

Kabir : From Siva.

Dattatreya : *From where is the Hang Sa produced?*

Kabir : From the Void.

Dattatreya : *From where is Brahma produced?*

Kabir : From Hang Sa.

Dattatreya : *From where is the Prana produced?*

Kabir : From Brahma.

Dattatreya : *From where is Sound produced?*

Kabir : From Prana.

Dattatreya : *From where is air produced?*

Kabir : From Sound.

Dattatreya : *From where is breath produced?*

Kabir : **From Air.**

Dattatreya : *From where is the mind produced?*

Kabir : **From breath.**

Chapter 6

How is The Mind Dissolved ?

Dattatreya : *How is the mind dissolved?*

Kabir : When the body dies, the mind dissolves in Air.

Dattatreya : *How is Air dissolved?*

Kabir : Air is dissolved in Sound.

Dattatreya : *How is Sound dissolved?*

Kabir : In Prana.

Dattatreya : *How is Prana dissolved?*

Kabir : **In Brahma.**

Dattatreya : *How is Brahma dissolved?*

Kabir : **Brahma is dissolved in Hang Sa.**

Dattatreya : *How is Hang Sa dissolved?*

Kabir : **Hang Sa is dissolved in the Void.**

Dattatreya : *How is the Void dissolved?*

Kabir : **The Void is dissolved in Omkar.**

Dattatreya : *How is the Omkar dissolved?*

Kabir : **It is dissolved in time.**

Dattatreya : *How is Time dissolved?*

Kabir : **Time is dissolved in jiva.**

Dattatreya : *How is jiva dissolved?*

Kabir : Jiva is dissolved in Siva (Tranquility).

Dattatreya : *How is Siva dissolved?*

Kabir : Siva is dissolved in Niranjana.

Dattatreya : *How is Niranjana dissolved?*

Kabir : Niranjana is dissolved in Niranjana.

At this state, the seeking self merges into the pure Self in Oneness. This is the eternal Realization, or eternal Life.

Both the sages remained silent for a while. Thereafter, *Yogi Dattratreya* withdrew himself from manifestation.

Kabir remained attuned in Oneness *Within.*

Chapter 7

The Conversation at a Glance

Dattatreya's Questions	Kabir's Answers
What is Mind?	Restless breath (Chanchal).
What is Air?	Union (Sandhi).
What is Sound?	Void (Sunya).
What is Prana?	Tranquility (Nirvana).
What is Brahma?	Grace (Kripa).
What is Hang Sa?	Eternity (Abinasi).
What is Time?	(Remains silent).
What is Void?	(Remains silent).
What is jiva?	Individuality.
What is Siva?	Tranquility.
What is Niranjana?	Unmanifested Self (Anupama).
Where does mind stay?	At the Heart (Hridaya).
Where does air stay?	At the Navel (Navi).
Where does Sound stay?	At Anahata.
Where does Prana stay?	In Fearlessness (Nirbhaya).
Where does Brahma stay?	In the Universe (Brahmanda).
Where does Hang Sa stay?	In the Sky (Gagana).
Where does Time stay?	In the Lotus (Kamal).
Where does Void stay?	In Unmanifestation (Anupa).
Where does Jiva stay?	In Air (Pabana).

Where does Siva stay?	In the Moon (Chandra).
Where does Niranjana stay?	In the Spinal Cord.

Dattatreya : *In the absence of their shelters, where do they stay?*

Kabir : Mind stays in Unmanifestation; air stays in the same; Sound stays Above; *Prana* stays in Eternity; *Brahma* stays in Himself, *Hang Sa* in Eternity, Time in Void, the Void in *Omkar*, the individual in Tranquility, Tranquility in Unmanifestation, Unmanifestation in Unmanifestation.

Dattatreya : *What is the essence of the mind and others?*

Kabir : The essence of mind is air; of air, renunciation and of renunciation, Sound. For Air (Breath), it is the same as above. For Sound, *Prana* is essence; for *Prana*, *Brahma*; for *Brahma*, *Hang Sa*; for *Hang Sa*, Eternity and the Void; for Eternity and Unmanifestation, the Void is essence; for Unmanifestation, Time; for time, individual being; for the Void, Unmanifestation; for individual being, Tranquility; for Tranquility (*Siva*), unmanifested Self (*Niranjana*) is essence and for Unmanifestation, One *Brahma*, or One Self is the essence.

Dattatreya : *From where are they produced?*

Kabir : Mind is produced from Air (Breath), Air from Sound, Breath from Air, Sound from *Prana, Prana* from *Brahma, Brahma* from *Hang Sa, Hang Sa* from the Void, Time from *Omkar*, the Void from Time, *jiva* from Siva, Siva from *Niranjana*, and *Niranjana* from the Fire (Mystic Fire). From the end, one after another is produced back to the mind.

Dattatreya : *How are they dissolved?*

Kabir : Mind dissolves in Air (Breath); Air in Sound; Sound in *Prana; Prana* in *Brahma; Brahma* in *Hang Sa* in the still state of Breath in meditation; and meditation resolves in *Omkar; Hang Sa* in *OM*; Time in Tranquility; Tranquility in Unmanifestation; Unmanifestation in Unmanifestation spontaneously and naturally by the Unmanifestation.

Chapter 8

The Spiritual Commentary

Remembering *Sri Guru*!

The word *Kabir* means *body*, and the word *Gita* means *whatever is sung at the After-effect-poise of Kriya in the name of eternal Realization*. *Yogi Kabir* was questioned by *Yogi Dattatreya* (an incarnation of Lord Siva) and *Kabir* replied to these questions.

Remembering the foregoing conversation, one attempt is made to explain it as far as possible.

Description is made through mind. All evolved from the mind and stays in the mind.

8.1   What is mind ?

When the breath does not stay tranquil, and it becomes restless, then it is called mind.

The speed of electricity is seen, but the speed of the mind is greater than electricity. Due to the great speed of the mind, things in front of things are seen.

The mind is moving always from one object to another. This is poisonous though the mind thinks of it as nectar. Thus, the mind attracts sufferings.

Without the practice of *Kriya* (which can be personally known from the Guru), mind, being restless breath, cannot be at rest, or at Peace.

The mind resides at the Heart which is in everything. Therefore, the tranquil mind, *Brahma*, the Self, is in everybody at the Heart. In absence of the Heart, Self stays in the unmanifested Form which is Unique and Absolute.

At the After-effect-poise of *Kriya (Kriyar-Parabastha)* and its Beyond (*Kriyar-Para-basthar-Para bastha*), all the *Kriyanwits* feel a kind of addiction of attunement.

The essence of the mind (restless breath) is Air. The still state of Breath is Purity, because, when the restless mind becomes tranquil, then it finds the Happiness and Peace.

The essence of Peace is renunciation, or detachment.

It is difficult to attain Peace without attaining the After-effect-poise of *Kriya* through the tranquil Breath.

The essence of renunciation, or detachment, is *Omkar*, the inner Sound, where the breath enters and dissolves. Fixing the mind perfectly at that state, one must not think of anything.

Tranquil Mind is produced by means of tranquil Breath (*Sthira bayu*), which is attained by the practice of *Pranayam*, or *Kriya*. From that tranquil Mind, the life Force (*Prana*), or breath, becomes tranquil.

The tranquil Mind is the Form of *Brahma* or the Self, which is a wonderful state. It is obvious and natural for people to know this state.

8.2   What is this state?

It is in the state of Union between life and death. The place is at Navel (*Navi*). When the Air, or Breath, does not stay at the navel, the *Niranjana* stays at *Kutastha* (in between the eyebrows) which is called luminous Heart (*Aditya Hridaya*). He is living in this body as *OM*. It can be realized by *Kriya* practice under the direct instructions from *Guru*, the Master.

The tranquil Air is produced from the Sound, *OM*. That Air is Breath, which is dissolved in that tranquil Air. It is like the Mother produced from *Brahma*. And air becoming *Brahma*, or the Self, dissolves in the ultimate Self at the After-effect-poise of *Kriya*.

The Sound is the Void. When the restless mind becomes tranquil, withdrawing from all sides, it stays in the Void (*Sunya*); then the Sound of *OM* is heard, and all the external Sounds dissolve into the Void, and striking the air, it starts rebounding.

Therefore, whatever you are hearing, all are the Void (*Sunya*). So *Brahma* is great Void, and thus, the Sound is *Brahma*.

This Sound stays at *Anahat* from where without any effort ten types of sound are produced.

For example, the sound of a fly, flute and a sitar are heard in the beginning.

Then come the sound of ringing bells, thunder, conchs, beating drums and metal brass plates and the roaring sound of a lion: these are the ten types of sound from *Anahat*, the luminous Heart. They stay at the Heart. All persons are in bondage to ordinary sound, so they listen to these ten types of sound.

Anahat is the Sound of *OM*, inner Sound, which is revealed by the practice of *Kriyas*. If it is heard by anyone, then one feels amazed, and finds the means to be freed from illusion (*Maya*: *Ma*, "inhaling"; *ya*, "exhaling," that is, breath).

Unfortunately, when one does not practice *Kriya*, or *Pranayam*, one goes deep down away from the Self.

When the Sound does not stay at *Anahat*, then it stays always in the Above, and the Clairaudience is heard in this Universe, that is, in the physical body. Clairaudience is held automatically without any effort.

The life of this inner Sound is *Prana*. Because without *Prana*, nothing is heard. The Sound is produced from *Prana* and is dissolved in *Prana*. That is, at the After-effect-poise of *Kriya*, Sound dissolves in *Brahma*.

The tranquil Air of *Prana* is the atom of *Brahma*, or the ultimate Self. The external manifestation of this atom is inner Light (*Jyoti*).

In a dark room, all are seen by the flash of light, and when illumination takes place in that atom, then one attains the Omniscient, Omnipotent and Almighty character. And the eightfold powers of *yoga* are automatically gained.

At the time of leaving the body, the person attains the state of Consciousness of whatever sentiment arises in this tranquil Air or *Prana*. This energy of *Prana* burns all limitations by the practice of *Kriya* at the After- effect-poise of *Kriya*.

8.3   What is *Prana*?

Prana is tranquil Air, or Breath in the tranquil Air, which produces *Nirvana*, eternal Tranquility.

All have fear of death, but *Brahma*, the ultimate Self has no death. Therefore, to be dissolved in *Brahma* is to be liberated while living in the physical body (*Jivanmukta*).

When *Omkar Kriyas* with *Talabya Kriya*, that is *Khecharimudra*, are practiced, the *Prana* is tranquilized in fearless unmanifested *Kutastha Brahma* (the ultimate Self); then there is no fear at all.

Jivanmukta, the absolute fearless liberated state, is the state of spontaneous Attunement.

If there is no Attunement, then *Prana* stays in eternal *Brahma*.

The Self is evolved from the Self, and is dissolved in the Self, like water dissolving in water.

Similarly, at the After-effect-poise of *Kriya*, the Self is in eternal Tranquility.

8.4   What is *Brahma* (the ultimate Self)?

Initiating into *Kriya* is the Grace of kindness as it brings Tranquility to the air, or breath, of individuals.

So, Grace is *Brahma*, or the ultimate Self.

In the absence of the physical body, *Brahma* stays in the supreme Being.

The life of *Brahma* is *Hang Sa*, because, if there were no *Hang Sa*, where would *Brahma* be?

Hang Sa is produced from *Hang Sa* as son produces son to become father.

Therefore, the life of *Brahma* is *Hang Sa* which dissolves in meditation.

Meditation is dissolved in *Omkar*. At that moment, the After-effect-poise of *Kriya* is *Brahma*.

Hang Sa is *Brahma* which is Eternal. *Hang Sa* is the Void in the Void.

In fact, He is truly *Brahma*. *Brahma* has no decay. Decaying means change of a state of manifestation. When there is nothing except ultimate Self, then how can there be another thing?

When there is One, this One is eternal, immortal *Hang Sa, Brahma*, the ultimate Self.

That embodiment of *Hang Sa (Kutastha Bindu*: the Divine Spot between the eyebrows) stays in the Sky (the ethereal Sky in the area between the eye-brows).

When there is no Sky, then *Hang Sa* stays in Eternity.

8.5 What is the essence of *Hang Sa*?

The essence of *Hang Sa*, or Eternity, is Void, and the essence of Void is Unmanifestation, the After-effect-poise of *Kriya*.

The essence of Unmanifestation is Time, because everything happens in time.

Hang Sa is produced from the Void and is dissolved in the body of *Omkar*, inner Sound. At the After-effect-poise of *Kriya* even the Void vanishes.

8.6 What is Time?

Time stays in the lotus. In the absence of the lotus, it stays in the Void. The life of time is individual being. Time is produced from the body of *Omkar*.

Time absorbs all manifestations, and thus is the destroyer.

But Tranquility absorbs even time, so Tranquility as Eternity is the Destroyer of the destroyer (time).

This Tranquility is the great ethereal Sky of Consciousness at the After-effect-poise of *Kriya*, as all melt there into One Consciousness.

8.7 Where does that Void stay?

The Void is in Unmanifestation of *Brahma*.

In the absence of unmanifested Self, it stays in the body of *Omkar*, inner Sound.

The life of the Void is Unmanifestation and is produced from Time, and it dissolves in the individual being at the After-effect-poise of *Kriya*.

The individual being stays at air, and in the absence of air (breath), he stays in Tranquility, as the life of individual being is Tranquility from where *Jiva*, or breath is produced and is dissolved.

When the individual being is dissolved in *Brahma*, then he becomes Tranquility.

Tranquility is the form of Moon which stays in the head In the absence 0f Moon (*Chandra*), *Kutastha* stays in Unmanifestation.

The Essence of Unmanifestation is Unmanifestation. Tranquility is produced from Unmanifestation and is dissolved in Unmanifestation.

8.8 Where does Unmanifestation (*Niranjana*) stay?

Niranjana (unmanifested Self) stays in the Spinal Cord.

In the absence of Spinal Cord, Unmanifestation stays in *Kutastha*. The Essence of Unmanifestation is One *Brahma*. Unmanifestation is produced from Fire, or Energy (tranquil Air, or Breath) and is being dissolve in its own Form automatically, or spontaneously, at the After-effect-poise of *Kriya*.

8.9 Summary

Among the above-mentioned eleven subjects let us remember once again:

1. the mind,

2. the air,

3. the Sound,

4. *Prana*,

5. *Brahma*,

6. *Hang Sa*,

7. Time,

8. the Void;,

9. *Jiva*, or the individual being,

10. *Siva*, or supreme Being, and

11. *Niranjana*, or the unmanifested Self.

Hang Sa is in the center of all the eleven, as Lord *Narayana*.

He is Eternity in His eternal aspect.

He becomes the individual being and is holding this world.

He is the all-pervading great ethereal Consciousness and unparalleled, because he has become all these things. For that reason, He is called the Lord of all (*Sarveshwar*).

From the Void, He makes all in time, and the Sound of Sky is dissolved in *Omkar*.

This inner Sound is spontaneous; one can listen just by concentrating on It.

When *Hang Sa*, the tranquil Breath, or Air, becomes restless, it becomes the mind.

When mind enters into the still state of Breath in the state of Union (*Sandhi*), it is called Air (*Pavan*).

When the air adhering to the Void enters in the Void itself, then the air is called Sound.

This Sound is *Omkar*. The tranquil state of this inner Sound is called *Nirvana* (Liberation, or the state of Freedom). Then air is called *Prana*.

Prana being kind to itself enters into *Brahma* and takes the name of *Brahma*.

In this physical body, mind, air, Sound, *Prana, Brahma, Hang Sa*, Time, Void. individual being (*jiva*), Siva (Tranquility, the supreme Being), and *Niranjana* (the unmanifested Self) reside respectively in the Heart, Navel, *Anahat*, Unmanifested world, Sky, Lotus, Air, Moon, and in the Spinal Cord.

In the absence of suitable shelter, they stay in *Anup/Anupam, Niranjana*, Above, Eternity, the Self, Eternity, the Void, *Omkar*, supreme Being or Tranquility, and *Niranjana*, respectively.

For want of which one cannot exist, it is called Essence, or Life.

For example, the essence of mind is Air, as the mind cannot exist without Breath.

And the essence of tranquil Air is renunciation. Without listening to the inner Sound, *Omkar*, the state of renunciation cannot last.

Therefore, *Prana* is the Essence of life. And apart from *Brahma*, there is no *Prana*. Therefore, the Essence of *Prana* is *Brahma*, Himself.

Without *Hang Sa* in the great ethereal Sky, there is no *Brahma*. So the Essence of *Brahma*, the ultimate Self, is *Hang Sa*.

Without Eternity, where is *Hang Sa*? Apart from the After-effect-poise of *Kriya*, where is the ethereal Sky of Consciousness? So, the Essence of Eternity is great Void.

Apart from the unmanifested Being who is Unique where is the great Void (ether)? So the essence of the great ethereal Sky of Consciousness is unmanifested infinite Self.

Apart from Time, where is the unmanifested Self? So the essence of Unmanifestation is Time. Where is time apart from the individual being? Hence, the essence of Time is the individual being.

Apart from the unmanifested Self, where is the Void? So, the essence of the Void is the unmanifested Self.

Wherever there is individual being, there is supreme Being, eternal Tranquility. So the essence of individual being is Tranquility, or pure Being.

The essence of Oneself (One *Brahma*) is the unmanifested Self at the After-effect-poise of *Kriya*.

There, the individual being becomes the *Kutastha*, the inner Self, because at that time the addiction of Attunement in Oneness (*Samadhi*) between the individual self and the pure Self is attained spontaneously.

All people talk about mind, but many do not know from where mind is produced.

The mind is produced from Breath, and is dissolved into tranquil Breath at the After-effect-poise of *Kriya*.

The tranquil Air is produced from *Omkar*, and breath is produced from Air which is dissolved in *Omkar*.

Omkar is produced and dissolved in *Prana*. *Prana* is produced and dissolved in the ultimate Self.

Brahma is produced and dissolved in the Void through meditation.

Time is produced from *Omkar* and is dissolved in time.

The Void is produced from time and is dissolved in the individual being which is produced from the supreme Being, Tranquility, and is dissolved in Tranquility.

Tranquility is produced and is dissolved in unmanifested Self.

Niranjana is produced from Fire, or Energy, and is dissolved in Fire (*Anil*) on its own, spontaneously.

8.10 The Eleven Subjects at a Glance

Produced from:	Dissolved in:
Mind from breath.	Air (tranquil Air).
Air from Sound and breath from Air.	Sound.
Sound from *Prana*.	*Prana*.
Prana from *Brahma*.	*Brahma*.
Brahma from *Hang Sa*.	*Hang Sa*, Meditation, and *Omkar*.
Hang Sa from the Void.	*Omkar*.
Time from *Omkar*.	Time.
The Void from time.	Individual being.
Individual from the supreme Being.	The Lord Siva, the supreme Being.
Lord Siva, or Tranquility, from *Niranjana*.	*Niranjana* (Unmanifestation).
Niranjana from Fire (*Anil*).	Fire (*Anil*), Energy automatically dissolved Within Itself.

One after another, the manifestations of the eleven subjects vanish, but the fundamental eleven elements remain: Mind, Air, Sound, *Prana, Brahma,* Meditation through *Hang Sa, Omkar*, Time, Siva, and *Niranjana*. He is in His own form and is in Himself by Himself.

The mind is in the inhaling. By the practice of *Kriya*, or *Pranayam*, the mind should be dissolved in tranquil Air, or Breath.

If mind is applied in the tranquil Breath, then one Sound is heard in low-high pitch.

Therefore, the Sound of *Omkar* is produced from *Prana*. So by practicing *Kriya*, or *Prana*, remaining always attuned by the practice of *Kriya*, one is dissolved in *Brahma*, the ultimate Self.

The self is dissolved in *Hang Sa* through meditation by the practice of *Pranayam* 1,728 times.

This *Omkar* is dissolved in the physical body. When one stays there in time, then eventually, one stays eternally, or dissolved in time, and he becomes Tranquility Itself.

Kutastha is dissolved in His own Infinite state, automatically and spontaneously, which is called *Soham Brahma*: That I am.

The scripture speaks of *Nijabodha-rupam*, or *Self Understanding.*

When the *Kriyanwit* holds to this state of Consciousness spontaneously Within Oneself by oneself, it is called absolute Knowledge (*Purna Jnana*).

Thus, he attains the absolute Freedom.

The End Of Kabir Gita

Om! Shanti! Shanti!! Shanti!!!

Other Books in Print

This is a a scriptural commentary of Lahiri Mahasaya on *The Avadhuta Gita* in the Light of *Kriya*. Lahiri Mahasaya is a polestar of Kriya Yoga, a direct disciple of Mahavataar Babaji. In previous birth, he was Kabir. He is the Sadguru of Saint Shirdi Sai Baba.

Avadhuta is a truly renunciate, realized and wandering *MahaYogi*. Ancient *MahaYogi Dattatreya*'s revelations to the world is *The Avadhuta Gita*. *Dattatreya* is considered by many as an incarnation of *Lord Shiva*.

Ancient Kriya Yoga Mission is engaged in disseminating simple techniques of ancient science of living. Every word uttered by a Yogi has a special meaning that is totally unintelligible to even the highly intellectual people. This book is written in such a way that everyone can follow it up while trading the path of Kriya. People think that they are very intelligent, but if they try to understand very seriously, they realize perfectly that nothing is happening according to their intellect.

Only those whose breath is not blowing in the left or right nostril are intelligent in this world.

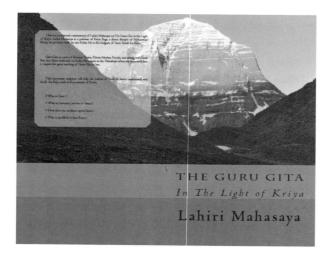

This is a a scriptural commentary of Lahiri Mahasaya on *The Guru Gita* in the Light of *Kriya*. Lahiri Mahasaya is a polestar of Kriya Yoga, a direct disciple of Mahavataar Babaji. In previous birth, he was Kabir. He is the Sadguru of Saint Shirdi Sai Baba.

Guru Gita is a part of *Biswasar Tantra*. Divine Mother, *Parvati*, was sitting with Lord Siva, her divine husband, on Kailas Mountain in the Himalayas when she requested him to impart the great teaching of *Guru Gita* to her.

This important scripture will help the seekers of Truth to better understand and clarify the Kriya path in their pursuit of Truth:

- Who is *Guru* ?

- What is *Guruseva* (service to *Guru*) ?

- How does one meditate upon *Guru* ?

- Who is qualified to have *Kriya* ?

**Drink Air Therapy
To Kill Diabetes**

A PATH TO SELF-CURE
AND IMMORTALITY

ANCIENT KRIYA YOGA MISSION

This book is written for preparing common mass to embrace a very simple but powerful self-help mechanism of drinking air(not breathing air) to eradicate Diabetes(both Type 1 and 2) from root and foster longevity with healthy body and mind.

These simple techniques are meant to be practiced by anyone without any external assistance and guidance.

This is a scriptural commentary of Lahiri Mahasaya on The Omkar Gita in the Light of Kriya in which God Krishna answers to Prince Arjuna about the Omkar.

Lahiri Mahasaya is a polestar of Kriya Yoga, a direct disciple of Mahavataar Babaji. In previous birth, he was Kabir. He is the Sadguru of Saint Shirdi Sai Baba.

This is a scriptural commentary of Lahiri Mahasaya on Kabir's couplets.

Lahiri Mahasaya is a polestar of Kriya Yoga, a direct disciple of Mahavataar Babaji. In previous birth, he was Kabir. He is the Sadguru of Saint Shirdi Sai Baba.

This is a scriptural commentary of Lahiri Mahasaya on The Upanishads. Lahiri Mahasaya is a polestar of Kriya Yoga, a direct disciple of Mahavataar Babaji. In previous birth, he was Kabir. He is the Sadguru of Saint Shirdi Sai Baba.

If we scan the word Upanisad, *we see that* Upa *means "sitting" and* nisad *means "near." Thus, the very word* Upanisad *specifies personal relationship: the Guru-param-para [Master to Disciple learning from the living lips of a Guru].*

In ancient times, the disciples sat near the Guru

to learn the spiritual discipline from the living lips of their Guru to realize the supreme Self. They practiced strictly in accordance with the instructor they received personally from the living lips of their Guru. This is a Kriya Yoga book intended to be read and practiced by everyone, with/without initiation.

Please note that the Guru here means the Kutastha, i.e., the place between the eyebrows, also known as The Third Eye.

Ancient Kriya Yoga Mission is engaged in disseminating simple techniques of ancient science of living. Every word uttered by a Yogi has a special meaning that is totally unintelligible to even the highly intellectual people. This book is written in such a way that everyone can follow it up while trading the path of Kriya. People think that they are very intelligent, but if they try to understand very seriously, they realize perfectly that nothing is happening according to their intellect.

Thoughts are inseparably related to breathing. So, when the number of breaths is reduced, thoughts are reduced proportionately.

Eventually, with the tranquilization of breath, thoughts are dissolved. Thereby, the seeker can attain the After-effect-poise of Kriya, or eternal Tranquility, which is Amrita, nectar proper.

This is a scriptural commentary of Lahiri Mahasaya on The Bhagavad Gita.

1. *Bisad Yoga : Arjuna's (Seeker's) Melancholy*

2. *Sankhya Yoga : Knowledge of the Self*

3. *Karma Yoga : Action*

4. *Jnan Yoga : Knowledge and Wisdom*

5. *Karma-Sanyas Yoga : Action and Renunciation*

6. *Avyas Yoga : Practice*

7. *Jnan-Bijnan Yoga : Knowledge and Realization*

8. *Akshara-Brahma Yoga : The Eternal Self*

9. *Raja Vidya Raja Gujya Yoga : The Supreme Science and The Supreme Secret*

10. *Bibhuti Yoga : The Divine Glories*

11. *Biswarupa Darsan Yoga : The Universal Form of The Self*

12. *Bhakti Yoga : Devotion*

13. *Kshetra and Kshetrajna : The Prakriti-Purusha Yoga*

14. *Gunatraya Bibhag Yoga : Threefold Qualities*

15. *Purushottam Yoga : The Supreme Person*

16. *Daibasura Sampad Bibhag Yoga : The Divine and Demoniacal Properties*

17. *Shraddhatraya Bibhag Yoga : The Threefold Respect*

18. *Moksha Yoga : Liberation*

This is a Kriya Yoga book intended to be read and practiced by everyone, with-/without initiation.

Every word uttered by a Yogi has a special meaning that is totally unintelligible to even the highly intellectual people.

This book is written in such a way that everyone can follow it up while trading the path of Kriya.

People think that they are very intelligent, but if they try to understand very seriously, they realize perfectly that nothing is happening according to their intellect.

Only those whose breath is not blowing in the left or right nostril are intelligent in this world.

When breathing is faster, then in one day and one night respiration can flow up to 113,680 times. Normally during the same time, the figure is 21,600 times. During a day and night, if respiration is faster than usual, the breath can flow in and out 113,680 times. Normally, in the course of a day and night, there are 21,600 breaths. This figure is reduced by Kriya practice to 2,000 times. So, breathing 1,000 times in the day and 1,000 times in the night, in a normal course, provides greater Tranquility to a Yogi. One of his breaths takes about 44 seconds. Such a Yogi is matured in Kriya practice.

Thoughts are inseparably related to breathing. So, when the number of breaths is reduced, thoughts are reduced proportionately. Eventually, with the tranquilization of breath, thoughts are dissolved. Thereby, the seeker can attain the After-effect-poise of Kriya, or eternal Tranquility, which is Amrita, nectar proper.

LAHIRI   MAHASAYA

This is a compilation of selected works of Lahiri Mahasaya.

1. *The Bhagavad Gita*

2. *The Omkar Gita*

3. *The Upanishads*

4. *Kabir's Dohe(Couplets)*